The Lost Art of Bel Canto

From the Studio of William L. Whitney

The Lost Art of Bel Canto

Leta Fulton Whitney

The Lost Art of Bel Canto by Leta Fulton Whitney

Copyright © 2016 by Andy Anselmo

All rights reserved, including the right to reproduce this book or portions thereof in any form whatsoever without written permission from the copyright owner or publisher.

For information about special discounts for bulk purchases, please contact the publisher.

Media Hatchery
P. O. Box 554
Orchard Park, NY 14127
716.245.1634

MediaHatchery.com
info@MediaHatchery.com

First paperback edition March 2016

Designed and edited by William C. Even
MediaHatchery.com

Music Restoration and Engraving by Schweibacher Music Preparation, Canandaigua, NY

Manufactured in the United States of America

Library of Congress Control Number: 2015960991

ISBN: 978-0-9971276-1-4 (paperback)

Contents

Foreword vii

Quotes ix

Introduction
    A Biographical Sketch of William L. Whitney 1

The Method
    Introduction 11
    The Instrument 13
    Tone Management and Production 14
    The Breath 16
    Diction 17
    Covered Tone 20
    When To Cover 21
    The Act of Singing 24
    Posture 26
    Pitch 27
    Registers 29

Studies and Exercises
    Studies 34
    Exercises
        For Developing Vocal Line 36
        For Controlling and Sustaining Tone 36
        For Maintaining Vocal Line with Changing Vowel Sound ... 37

>   For Breath Management 38
>   For Messa di Voce.. 40
>   For Developing the Trill 41
>   For Developing Flexibility for Florid Passages 42
>   For the Use of:
>   1. Graded Breath Pressure... 43
>   2. Covered and Normal Tone 43
>   3. Cross of the Voice... 43
>   For Handling the Breath... 44
>   Scale Endings 45
>
> BABBO 46

Foreword

The Lost Art of Bel Canto is the most important modern work I have ever read on the subject of the *bel canto* method of singing. First, it tells the story of the life of William Lincoln Whitney, my beloved teacher of this technique and how he learned from his father and from the greatest masters in Europe in the late years of the 19th century, and then taught thousands of pupils, including the great Eleanor Steber. Mr. Whitney gave his last lesson in December, 1949 and died a week later. I was studying with him at that time at the New England Conservatory of Music in Boston, Massachusetts.

Mr. Whitney had begun writing the story of his life, basing himself on notes from an interview. This was completed by his widow, the late Leta Fulton Whitney, in 1954. It is charming, amusing, and impressive—a rare and unbeatable combination. Their son, William II, has contributed his touching reminiscences of his father's family, from letters going back to the early years of the 19th century, and a number of surprising (to me) revelations of his family's life as seen by the little boy and young man he became.

The materials on the *bel canto* method itself, as taught by Mr. Whitney, are from his personal notes and mark-ups of music. Mrs. Whitney had been his pupil, totally grasped everything about the method, and went on to teach the method herself.

In 1938, I became the pupil of Louise E. Sleep at the *First Settlement Music School* in Buffalo, New York. She had studied with Mr. Whitney, and from very early in our association, insisted I had to go to Boston and study *bel canto* with him. With hard work and sacrifice, I was able to do it and my life truly began at the moment I walked into his studio. These were the happiest years of my life, from September, 1945, through December, 1949. I earned my Bachelor's and Master's degrees in music at the New England Conservatory of Music and went on to a career in show business, using my *bel canto* technique. I began to teach some pupils in the mid-1960s and gradually I realized my happiest times were when I taught. While I still performed, I established the *Singers Forum*, a non-profit foundation in New York City, and finally, consciously, realized that I was carrying on Mr. Whitney's teaching, as he carried on his father's.

Between the Whitneys and myself, we have taught the *bel canto* technique for nearly a hundred and fifty years!

I became determined to find a way to publish the method, and in 1999, through the Conservatory, was able to contact Mr. Whitney's son. I was overjoyed when he told me of the unpublished manuscript written by his parents. Once my autobiography, *A Star-Crossed Life*, was finished, it became my personal mission to get this wonderful book published, and here it is!

I leave you with my favorite instruction to my own students: "Enjoy and learn."

— *Andy Anselmo*

Quotes

I've tried to learn to sing from 35 voice teachers from America to England, France and Italy. But Andy produced sounds from me I had been waiting all my life to make.
— *José Ferrer*

I'd always wanted to sing but thought there was no way I could. But with Andy's teaching, I now have a singing art that still stays in perfect order. I'm performing all over the country with "Street Songs," and even the White House, and it's all entirely his doing. If I were to wish for something to happen to someone that I love, I'd wish that at sometime in their life, they would be this lucky. I love him very much.
— *Geraldine Fitzgerald*

Andy sings the words like Frank Sinatra does.
— *Julie Harris*

Andy is a male Barbra Streisand.
— *Phyllis Diller*

When Andy sings, the angels curtsy.
— *Liza Minnelli*

Andy is the best of the best. What great times together! Thanks.
— *Regis Philbin*

Andy: thank you for fixing my voice.
— *Saundra Santiago*

You will never know just how much I love you ... but I'm trying!
—*Rue McClanahan*

The Lost Art of Bel Canto

Everybody searches for some kind of enlightenment in every field. As far as singing goes, it's definitely Andy Anselmo.
— *Liza Minnelli*

Andy is the most wonderful, generous man anyone could hope to keep them in shape for whatever their voice or their life is doing to them.
— *Mandy Patinkin*

There is no place like the Singers Forum ... it combines an atmosphere of hard work with an abundance of joy.
— *Mariette Hartley*

In all my years of show business, I have never encountered a more productive system for the training of the voice.
— *Regis Philbin*

Introduction

A Biographical Sketch of William L. Whitney

In presenting this method, I am finishing a work started by William L. Whitney. In response to countless requests by students, friends, and strangers who have listened to his pupils during the past seventy-five years and have recognized in their beauty of voice and production the hand of a master teacher, I have tried to bring to you a faithful record of his convictions regarding voice training. For the validity of his method I make no brief, but suggest only that no other teacher of our day has so consistently turned out fine singers over so long a period. His modesty is well known and he would frown upon any effort to force his opinions upon anyone. It is in such a spirit that this work is undertaken. The reader is welcome to take it or leave it, for truth is not dependent upon acceptance by the many. Mr. Whitney and I spent long and happy hours together in the preparation of this book and though, due to his sudden death, it has fallen to me to do the actual writing, the content is strictly his.

Would you like to know something about the life and preparation of this man who has become so great a teacher? He was born in Boston on January 11, 1861, the son of Myron Whitney and Eleanora Breshea Whitney. For a resume of his life, I shall quote his own words, written down in dreadful anticipation of an interview with Mr. Rudolf Elie of the Boston Herald. (The interview turned out to be very pleasant and Mr. Whitney thoroughly enjoyed a two-hour session with the "Roving Reporter" while the bench outside his studio filled to overflowing with students waiting for their lessons.)

> I resided on Summer Street, then a residential section, now usurped by the bargain basements, hardware and eating establishments—in short, business.
>
> In my trundle bed I was given my first example of *Messa di voce*, by what I later found to be one of the most beautiful, cultivated bass voices in the world—my father's.

Business drove us out of Summer Street, but as music still held our interest and a new music school was establishing itself nearby (The New England Conservatory of Music), I was enrolled as a piano student with B. J. Lang. This was in the late [eighteen] sixties in the old Music Hall Building on Winter Street.

When I reached the recital-playing stage, Mr. Lang removed me to his private class—not because of my great promise, but, I am sure, because of the hopelessness of making a silk purse out of a sow's ear. (The "sow's ear stage" is still upon me in spite of the eighty years of struggle during which I have nearly filled a borrowed silk purse.)

My father's oratorio and concert engagements abroad obliged us to move to England where I was placed in the *Beringer School for the Higher Development of Pianoforte Playing* to study both composition and piano under Mr. Oscar Beringer (London, 1874). One of the greatest experiences in these years was the opportunity to attend many rehearsals of great works with the greatest musicians of the day as soloists. Such performances have seldom been equaled and never surpassed.

A few years in London convinced me that music was beyond me; that practicing was the most useless and torturing thing in the world; that I would have no more of it. The grandest thing in the world was business with great ships sailing the seas gathering sheckles and treasure from all countries. I forgot to count the stages between merchant and errand boy in Whitley's Emporium (where everything from a needle to a white elephant could be bought). My reading had taken in accounts of American sailing ships and their astounding accomplishments, including downing the Mediterranean pirates and overcoming the opposition of Japan to foreign trade, etc.

Home again to America, my business career was started by two of Boston's successful businessmen and friends of my father, who took an interest in my newfound ambition and offered to try me out in their stores. First, Mr. Eben Jordan, who placed me in a department adjoining his office where he could keep an eye on me. He sometimes tried me out on some small affair supposedly within my reach. As I was obviously not a glowing success; he changed me to the wholesale department—a bad move as it was then summer and, of course, summer meant vacation. It was considered rather too soon for a vacation, but one was nevertheless granted. However, at the end of two weeks, a broken ankle necessitated more weeks of vacation. On my return, Mr. Jordan thought that business was perhaps not my chief talent and advised my going elsewhere.

Mr. Oliver Ditson thought there might be added interest in his business as I had spent some time in the study of music. The year I spent in Ditson's has been beneficial in many ways. I gained considerable knowledge of the publishing of music, made the acquaintance of much good music and saw quite clearly how long it remained on the shelves in the basement without selling.

Ditson was the agent for Steinway Piano and the great pianists of the world came to the piano room to practice for their recitals. The hours I spent listening did not benefit Ditson's music store business, but it did revive my interest in music. By borrowing a couple of dollars to add to my weekly pay of three dollars, I was able to renew my piano lessons. William Sherwood was my teacher. I did rather well, but unfortunately I began to sing, and people here and there thought it sounded like my father's voice. (It should be noted that people think a good many things that are not so.) At that time Gilbert and Sullivan were producing some mighty interesting works which led some influential Bostonians to the idea of producing an opera called *Pinafore*.

By engaging the most distinguished singers and forming a chorus entirely of church choir singers, the new venture could be tried with a prospect of success. So with Adelaide Phillips, my father, Tom Karl (an experienced tenor), Barnabee for the brighter side, and others, the venture met with great success.

Zerahn's son was my fellow-employee at Ditson's so we asked the Opera Manager to take us into the chorus. We were taken. My salary of three dollars became nineteen dollars as the opera paid us the astonishing salary of sixteen dollars per week. That was all very well as long as the company stayed in Boston, but when they went on tour it became necessary for Zerahn and me to resign our positions at Ditson's. I am afraid we were both all too easily spared.

A year or so of singing with the Company, and then attention was being paid to my voice. For some years I had been playing for my father's practice—*The Messiah*, *Elijah*, Bach's *Passions*, and all the repertory basses use the world over. This work taught me to sing properly with the right tone-production, proper phrasing, style, etc.

One morning I received orders from my parents that I was to sail for Italy on the following Saturday. The entire Opera Company was at the steamer and gave a farewell concert which made me a marked man for that voyage.

Luigi Vannuccini, my father's teacher in Florence, Italy, was one of the very great teachers. He had been trained from boyhood up—a member of the Grand Duke's household; pianist, violinist, composer, and an excellent conductor. He was the first to conduct *Faust* in Italy. Gounod himself came to Italy to superintend the preparations, going over the score note for note with Vannuccini. (It was sung in Italian.) Vannuccini was closely associated with Bellini, Donizetti, Rossini, Verdi, and conducted their operas with a knowledge of their wishes, which is possible only through personal association. He wrote the cadenzas for many of the greatest singers of the day and coached them in their various parts. It was due to his kindness that I was permitted to meet all the great composers and musicians with whom he worked, and to be a member of the group during discussions of how the various works should be sung.

Vannuccini's own teacher of voice was Romano, a noted teacher of the 1820's or 1830's. Vannuccini received his instruction while his voice was that of a boy soprano. He did not sing after the change, but as a teacher he could do the most astonishing things with no voice, *mezzo voce* and *sotto voce*. His pupils were many of the great. He molded the voices into the pattern intended by nature. Scalchi Zavas was a product of his work, he sharing with Adelina Patti the honors in the performance of *Semiramide* which was called for in all the countries of the civilized world. Vannuccini taught Patti's first husband, Nicollini, at the latter's home for a time, but as Nicollini's one-room "apartment" was a bedroom at night, and unfortunately, part of the day (Nick's wife remaining in bed behind discreet curtains during the lessons), the piano also served for a sideboard and dressing table and soon was unavailable for lesson giving, so Nick journeyed to the Vannuccini home.

Many Americans studied with Vannuccini. He married one of them, a Bostonian. George Sweet worked with him during my stay in Italy. My father was one of his most noted pupils, and he never tired of singing the praises of his teacher. His particular kindness and tireless work with me, I attribute to his great regard for my father and love of his wonderful voice.

It was my good fortune to have seven years of work on my voice with him, resulting in the understanding of the things necessary to consider in the training of voices, as well as definite rules applicable to all voices in the forming of what is called *method* to build on. The results of this work were evidenced much later.

In 1884 an event at this time—May 4—called for a temporary change of program. A wedding in Italy which took two days and four ceremonies: English Consulate, American Consulate, Palazzo Vecchio, Hall of the Mayor, and finally, the English Church with Lohengrin and offerings by the American Singers, some of whom became famous artists. A voyage to America, then back to Italy and on to Germany; Munich for composition with Rheinberger and Wagnerian Opera with Hoff Kapelmeister Fischer. For classmates in Munich I had Horatio Parker, Arthur Whiting, Woller, of the Bethlehem Choir, Schirmer's son-in-law White, and for a time, Philip Hale.

It seemed wise to do a season's work with Stockhausen and so we left for Frankfort. I studied German Lieder, Bach, Handel, and Brahms. Bach and Handel I had had with my father but it was interesting to approach the works again with another great master of singing. Stockhausen and Brahms were great friends, the latter dedicating the Lieder to Stockhausen. Stockhausen arranged a meeting for me with Brahms and a friendship began which was to be an everlasting joy to me. I was fortunate to be so associated for it gave me an understanding of Brahm's wishes and intentions regarding his music.

Many concert appearances in Munich, Leipsig, etc. While in Munchen, the great event—a son (almost lost his right to vote in America by being born on foreign soil. The Bostonian managed to figure it out in a couple of years and he was permitted to help elect the wrong man.)

Piano with B. Buonamici, Composition with Sir Alexander MacKenzie, Opera with Scheggi, Voice with Vannuccini, Violin with Faini, as well as concert engagements, kept me busy in the late 1880's in Florence. Florence was a wonderful place for musicians and artists in those days. A group of American artists, dissatisfied with the art work in Munich, begged a great American painter, Duveneck, to take them to Florence. He consented and this group of painters joined a group of musicians, to which I luckily belonged. Almost any evening would find us gathered at the home of a Florentine or American family where we sang songs and arias, played solos, two-piano music and parts from operas. Opera performances found us all in attendance for a few soldi, and it was a common occurrence to hear the entire audience singing the arias at the top of their voices as they started for home.

In the late [eighteen] eighties, the American Opera Company conducted by Theodore Thomas, then the leading opera company in America, sent me a contract whereby I was to alternate with my father in his roles. Stockhausen advised me to decline this offer and to go instead to England. This I did, and after filling concert and oratorio engagements at more than one of which the entire royal family was present, I was invited to teach at the *Royal College for the Blind* in Suydenham. It was during this stay in England that I sang for Edward VII, then Prince of Wales. My nervousness got the best of me and I trembled and shook through Beethoven's "Adelaide." Edward clapped vociferously and invited me to sing the song again as it was his favorite. The second time through, the nervousness gave way and the results were more nearly fit for the King that this fine man was.

During my stay in London I was invited to sing a solo part in Liszt's *Saint Elizabeth*, which Sir Alexander MacKenzie had prepared for the occasion of Liszt's coming to England for his great Jubilee. The entire nation did him honor at that time.

Several years of teaching in the Wimbledon School followed. The Kaiserine, daughter of Queen Victoria, had attended this school and on her return to England for her mother's Golden Jubilee, I was called upon to sing in a palace concert given for her entertainment. Queen Victoria and the entire family with close friends and visiting officials made up the audience.

Declining a professorship at the Royal College, I returned to Boston to teach at the New England Conservatory, at the same time filling various concert engagements throughout the country. However, I found that the teaching demanded so much of my time and attention that it would be wiser to be either a singer or a teacher, but not both. After some consideration, teaching won out. I have not sung since, but have devoted myself to the training of singers.

In 1900 I left the Conservatory and started my own school, *The William L. Whitney International School For Vocalists and Pianists*. For some years I had been taking some of my most promising pupils to Florence during the summer months to work with Vannuccini and Buonamici and decided to devote all my time to a school of my own. There were branches of my school in Paris, Florence, New York and Boston, each with faculties representing the leading musicians of the day. These were great days, as the hundreds of enrolled pupils would bear witness. Before starting my own school, Louise Homer studied with me as my own private pupil.

Around 1920 I was urged to return to the Conservatory and have been teaching there ever since.

1928 was a banner year for on December 22, I had the unbelievable good fortune to become the husband of my favorite pupil, and in 1930 our son, William L. Whitney II, was born. At this writing he is in his first year at Yale and his mother is receiving her Master's degree at Harvard. You can see that I am caught in the middle of a collegiate struggle.

The interesting and rewarding events of my life, crowned with this personal happiness, are entirely undeserved but gratefully acknowledged.

The modesty characteristic of Mr. Whitney forbids that he dwell on his own accomplishments as an artist in all three fields of composition, voice, and piano, and in deference to that modesty, I will simply say that George W. Chadwick told me that he rated many of his compositions as outstanding among American composers. As a concert singer, he was in demand throughout Europe, England, and America, and was soloist with most of the great oratorio societies of the world. As a pianist, he preferred the field of accompaniment in which he was unexcelled. Anyone whom he accompanied felt that his playing was like an orchestra under him. His sensitive musicianship, thorough and remarkable musical education, and vast experience gave him authority in style and interpretation of the composer, as well as in the actual production of the voice. For those who knew him, the white cotton "policeman" gloves which he wore both at practice and performance (the ivory of piano keys poisoned his fingers) were a constant source of amusement and all of us marveled that in so cumbersome an attire, those fingers could so delicately and surely produce accompaniments of such unrivaled brilliance, clarity, and wit.

In the studio, Mr. Whitney never sang to demonstrate what he wished the pupil to do. "No one ever heard him say, "Do it like this," or "Make it sound like this." Instead, he indicated on the keyboard and by facial expression and gesture, the stress and release, the rhythmic contour, and the management of the breath that produced the desired placement of the tone. The eloquence of these gestures coupled with the careful marking of every exercise, vocalise, or song will never be forgotten by those of us who were so fortunate as to have been his pupils. The reason for this approach was that he taught by a method—not just a hit or miss "do as I do"—and realized that unless the pupil understood when he achieved a good tone and how it was achieved, that pupil would never be an artist, but always one who mimicked and so needed a mentor.

The lessons were always stimulating and exciting, for each pupil was a new and individual problem, demanding the different exercises and varying emphases supplied from a fabulous store of exceedingly musical and attractive vocalizzi supported by delicious original accompaniments that made one's mouth water. Many of these exercises were figures taken from early compositions, unknown to most people today, and many were made up on the spur of the moment to fill a vocal need which his keen ear discerned. His use of arias from very early Italian operas and songs from the Italian Antiche as vehicles for vocal development gave the pupil the satisfaction of having "pieces" from the earliest lessons without in any way disturbing the foundational work of voice placement and management upon which every lesson centered. Later on, these same arias often served pupils in their concert programs and came to the public as charming and beautiful numbers new to its ears. Lessons were also enhanced by the rare and quick wit for which Mr. Whitney was justly famous. The keenest of us could not keep up with him, and many a time the hidden meaning of a remark was realized long after the lesson was finished.

Honesty and generosity went hand in hand in his approach to all musicians. No one was promised anything, and no one was encouraged to study in hope of "making the Met," or of being a concert singer in six months, or a year, or at all. If there was joy to be had for a student in developing the voice to the limits of its potential, then that student was acceptable. He never even promised *himself* success for any pupil, though many showed unmistakable indications of ultimate success.

The beginner was more interesting to him than the experienced singer and countless of the latter were refused in favor of young voices as yet undeveloped. The infinite care with which these voices were handled and the patience with which he guided both voice and student bespoke his generosity of spirit and his devotion to the true art of beautiful singing.

I have purposely omitted the names of any pupils, for to name some as successful because they became world famous and to omit those who were also successful at a different rung on the ladder would be to suggest a discrimination which he would not countenance. Suffice it to say that his available records show over four thousand pupils and that those who have not been a credit to their art may be counted on the fingers of two hands.

Dr. Harrison Keller, then President of the New England Conservatory of Music, paid tribute to Mr. Whitney at a Memorial Assembly held at the Conservatory on January 5, 1950, nine days after his sudden death. I cannot conceive of anything which would more truly or more beautifully express the man who gives reason for this book to be written. I quote Dr. Keller with deep appreciation:

> We have assembled this morning to honor and pay tribute to the memory of a man who has already become almost a legend, our beloved colleague, teacher, and friend, William L. Whitney, who for so many, many years has brought glory and distinction to his art and the School.
>
> The difficult task falls upon me of trying to express, however inadequately, our sense of irreparable loss—deep personal loss as well as the shattering loss to the Conservatory. I might dwell at length on what his going takes from us, but I prefer to remind you of some of the priceless values he leaves with us—the characteristics so indelibly fastened in our memories.
>
> His boundless energy, his indefatigable spirit and dignity; the exacting demands he made upon himself; his intolerance of sham and the mediocre, yet endless patience with, and encouragement for, worthy youth; his wonderful smile which reflected a world of kindness and understanding his pungent and penetrating criticism, always softened by a whimsical and delicious humor; the

wisdom and just decisions he contributed to the Faculty Council; and finally, the vast accumulation of knowledge and experience in his art which he poured so endlessly into the minds and hearts of generations of pupils ensuring the perpetuation of this great art for the years to come.

To us teachers and students he leaves then a rare model of maintaining complete and absolute integrity in his art and work—a perfect example of a career which, by his selfless desire to give out, regenerated perpetually his great spirit. Who of us, at the end of a career, would not prize his reward above most to have it said of him, as we can so justly say of our departed friend—he was a great artist, an inspired teacher, a devoted friend, and a good man.

— Leta Fulton Whitney

The Method

Introduction

Since the object of any voice method is to develop competent singers, it might be wise to begin our thinking together with a consideration of what makes a competent singer. Too often it is supposed that a fine natural voice and a good singer are synonymous, but such is far from correct. The fine natural voice is desirable, though there have been more than a few successful singers whose voices were little better than average, and there have been many more who, though magnificently endowed in their instrument, have failed to become successful singers. Though perhaps not commonly accepted, the human voice is an instrument demanding as skilled a player as is demanded for any other instrument. A Stradivarius violin is mute without the player and can be unbeautiful in the hands of a poor player. So it is with the human voice. The development of the ability to use the voice well involves placement, management, and the cultivation of an ear which will identify good and bad tone.

If only if were possible to describe *good tone*, much would be immediately accomplished, but such is not the case. However, an analysis of *musical* tone is within our grasp. In the little child, good tone is the natural tone, and the way to secure it is to eliminate anything which interferes with its free and spontaneous emission. This good tone is light, free, and clear, unforced, and free of affectation. Such tone is secured by eliminating poor posture, by encouraging the child to make light, sweet sounds to go with the words; by insisting on good diction, by keeping the voice within the easy range on the treble staff, and by encouraging the enjoyment of singing. Only rarely does one *teach* a little child to sing, and wisdom forbids that we approach the elimination of any bad singing habits through formal teaching.

With the adult, the production of good tone is also the elimination of poor singing habits, but it is a more formal and involved process. The adult, unlike the child, has become a complex bundle of physical, emotional, and psychological habits, many of which must be changed in order to *allow* the person to produce a naturally free, clear, light tone. With maturity comes a richer quality of tone—still natural, but quite different from the pure, white, almost transparent tone of the child. This mature voice is less easily handled than the child voice, and best results usually come through study of a formal nature, involving the development of ear and voice, through working with a competent teacher. This teacher will have a method or way of singing which will facilitate the production of good tone.

Such methods are based upon rules and concepts which, though important and well known to the teacher, are often obscure and indeed unknown to the pupil.

Any rule is an observation which has been found to be consistently useful and used by reason of its producing the desired end. Rules for harmony are not just something arbitrarily laid down by the teacher, but are the codifications of the success which I here try to explain. The rules which I shall set down are evolved from the art of the greatest singers and teachers of history and are stated as rules solely in an effort to clarify the way in which that art can be emulated. Any rules then, are merely a means to an end and not the end in themselves, and so will be used only in an effort to produce what the ear will recognize as good tone.

Once that has been sufficiently accomplished, the adherence to the rules becomes a *manner of singing* rather than a technical approach, and the artist begins to evolve.

Though it takes but a few words to outline, let us remember that the road to good tone-production is long and demanding, but ultimately rewarding.

It is not enough that the singer handle the voice skillfully. There is also the need for musicianship if one is to be a singer. The ability to read music (both rhythm and melody) is often the deciding point between the success and failure of two equally endowed singers. An acquaintance with and at least a practical command of the piano is an immeasurable asset to the singer. Skill at the keyboard is proportionately advantageous.

Languages—be they one's own or foreign—must be mastered, not just in academic approach, but as a medium of understanding, through precise and correct diction and conversational ability.

And now we come to that nebulous quality without which no musician attains the heights. We might call it interpretative ability which breaks down into a musical intelligence capable of divining the meaning of the music and projecting it so sensitively that the hearer shares in that interpretation.

To be a competent singer, it is essential that the individual be at home with a large repertory, thoroughly acquainted with the various styles, and capable of presenting each justly.

Even with this very brief and sketchy summary of the demands upon the singer, it is not difficult to see why so many beautiful voices are heard on all sides, yet few are capable of public careers. It is only fair, however, that we remember that membership in a leading opera company is not the essential accomplishment of all successful singers. In an economy such as ours in the United States, the opportunity for singing in a professional opera company is so limited as to be almost prohibitive, especially when our leading opera companies draw singers from the world market and still give preference to foreign singers. The most demanding and revealing of all mediums of the art of singing is through concert and oratorio work. In field of lieder singing, much neglected at present, lies the greatest subtlety of artistic expression. In this field, opportunity runs the gamut from small gatherings in the home town to engagements in the great halls throughout the world. Most of those who read this book will never be nationally known but if the student can follow patiently and meticulously, the path of developing good habits of voice-production and artistic growth, he will know the joy of competent singing.

The Instrument

The voice is a part of all normal people, and as such, it is taken for granted to the extent that few realize that it is an instrument as truly as any mechanically conceived music-maker. Since the voice, unlike other instruments, cannot be handled, taken apart, mechanically adjusted, or objectively studied, it remains a mystery. Many books and papers have been written about the anatomy of the voice, with minute attention to muscular and anatomical analysis, but no anatomist has ever produced a beautiful singer. It is the firm belief of Mr. Whitney after many years of signal success in the art of voice building, that the study of the anatomical and muscular aspect of the voice is detrimental to the student, for it leads to confusion, false emphasis, and tension. It is, however, necessary that the student recognize the vocal instrument and so, more from the point of interest than of value, let us compare this marvelous thing called the voice with other instruments with which we are visually and manually familiar.

The violin has strings, resonance cavity, and is played by a bow. The voice has strings called vocal cords, resonance cavities and bellows (lungs), and is played by the breath.

The violin has fixed, unchangeable position for its parts—strings, resonance chambers—and is played by a performer. The voice is played by the instrument itself and has movable cavities which must be manipulated by the instrument itself. The voice also has an ear attachment which requires development, for the ears are often tone-blind, sometimes tone-ignorant and only occasionally tone-keen.

The violin is mechanically adjusted and ready for the performer to play. The voice must be subjectively adjusted, not only to produce a satisfactory quality of tone for performance, but for every change in quality required by music.

Tone Management and Production

The violin is a queer-shaped box and we know that the cavity within the box gives us the resonance chamber by virtue of which we have the tone quality rather than a mere squeak when the bow is drawn over the strings. Actually, this cavity beautifies, adds fullness, quality, and loveliness to the tone produced by bow and strings, providing that the cavity is correctly shaped, the wood and varnish are the right kind and age, and the bar exactly placed.

Does the voice have a comparable resonance chamber? Yes, but there is not only one, but several such chambers. There are the mouth, the pharynx, the nasal cavities, the frontal cavity, and many other cavities in the head ("We try to avoid too many." —W. L. W.) Even the bones are resonance carriers as witnessed by the hearing aid given by pressing against the bone behind the ear.

To place a tone means to put it in a certain place. The violin needs no tone placing for its tone is mechanically fixed, as the parts of the violin are established and never change their relationships.

With the voice, however, it is essential that it be placed, and that the place must be made specific to the desired tone, for the parts are not in fixed relationship. We can do many things with the tongue, root of the tongue, and other functioning muscles, which will prevent the sound from reaching the resonance cavities. The contraction or stiffening of any muscle not concerned in the tone-production can and does interfere with the sound reaching the resonance cavities.

The resonance chambers themselves, with the exception of the chest, constantly change their position by virtue of changing head position, and it becomes necessary to place or adjust the cavities in order to produce the required tone quality suitable to the subject of the song, or the build of the melody.

The violin has four strings of varying thickness. Every note produced by the violin has its own string, varying in thickness and/or length according to the pitch desired. This is determined by the position of the stop or finger on the string best fitted to produce a specific pitch.

The voice has two strings or vocal cords which must serve the same purpose. They are really bands, the edges of which are made to vibrate by the breath. These bands, about 3/4 inch long, protrude from the two sides of the larynx or voice box. When vocal sounds are produced, the two edges meet, and the air passing through the narrow space causes the band edges to vibrate. When breathing, the bands which are joined at one end, spread apart but fly together when producing sounds. As the pitch rises, the cords are stretched. At a certain pitch, to avoid forcing, the cords join together at the free end and become thinner. Later, at higher pitch, they close up, leaving only a small opening. These various positions of the cords are often referred to as registers and would look something like this:

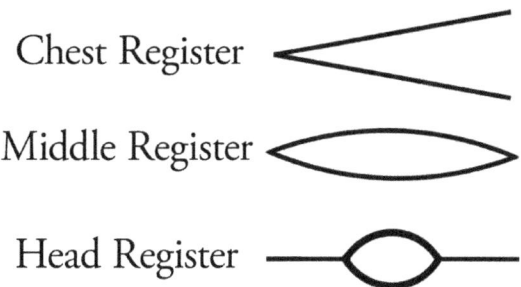

While this knowledge of the vocal cords is in no way essential to the singer, it is sometimes interesting and enlightening to the curious and may help to clarify the ensuing discussion of registers.

The Breath

The breath "plays" the voice as the bow plays the violin. Since all of us have been breathing rather successfully for a good many years, and only a few turn out to be good singers, there must be some particular way of breathing essential to the playing of the singing voice, and there is.

In ordinary breathing you will notice three evidences of inhaling. Sometimes you take a breath and your chest swells up like a pouter pigeon. Again, you breathe when you are relaxed or sleeping and the abdomen gets rounder and rounder, and still again at times you can feel your sides expand. That makes three kinds of breathing, two of which are used in singing. The eliminated one is the chest breathing. The chest serves its purpose as a resonance chamber.

Deep breathing, called *diaphragmatic*, *abdominal*, or *low*, is used in connection with side breathing, called *rib*, *intercostal*, or *lateral*. In imagination, or better, in sensation, the whole torso is an empty space entirely devoted to containing the breath. Consequently, the first movement of the inhalation is a descent of the breath to the abdominal region. The second is a slight expansion of the lower ribs. It is unwise take a capacity breath unless the phrase or build of the melody really demands it, since the act of singing demands that the breath be metered out, not wasted, and it is difficult to adequately restrain a super-abundance of breath. In the act of singing, the sensation should be one of lifting the breath, not pushing it up. The expulsion of breath is, of course, due to the action of the diaphragm, but conscious attention to that muscle usually results in a stiffening which in turn produces a squeezing, rather than a lifting, of the breath. The action of the diaphragm is accomplished through the inflation and deflation of the lungs. It is raised by the lateral expansion of the chest, not by the contraction of the abdominal muscles. Every inhalation is begun by a deflation of the lungs but that deflation must be simultaneous with the dropping of the diaphragm. The breath is not let out in a *whoof*, but is metered out to meet the need of the phrase or melody. One of the real arts of singing is the ability to so control the exhalation of the breath that only the needed amount passes through the vocal cords. This must be done without any sensation of tension or effort to restrain. It might be wise to add that the breath in singing is taken through the *mouth*, partly because more air can be inhaled more quickly in this way and partly because the act of breathing through the nose automatically closes the throat and often throws the voice out of position.

There is one other aspect of breathing which is basic to the voice production as taught by the masters. It is called *mounting the breath*, or in Italian, where you most often see it referred to, *montare il fiato*. It simply means raising the breath and perhaps can best be illustrated by a homely simile. Take a low breath, lift the breath up into the chest. This will draw the abdomen in. What did that do to the air? "It raised it from the kitchen to the second story without raising the roof," (— W. L. W.) to be used from the higher position, instead of the lower. This is a most helpful action in singing and will be applied and its use explained under tone management.

Diction

Two factors are involved in pronunciation—namely enunciation and articulation. The former is a matter of vowel sounds, while the latter involves the clarity and precision of speaking the consonants. Both are of utmost importance in singing, but enunciation is first as it is the vehicle for tone. Our language system is made up of two types of sound: vowels, or the sounds upon which the voice sustains, and consonants, the sounds which usually stop and start the vowels and which give the contrasting accompaniment to the sustaining sounds that we call words.

In singing, the vowels are the molds into which tone is poured to produce the different basic sounds. For the singer, they are not the English vowels: *a, e, i, o, u,* for these involve double vowels or diphthongs and so are not pure. Instead, the singer uses the pure molds of the Italian vowels, namely, *i* (mi), *e* (re), *a* (fa), *o* (do), and *u* (ut). These examples are as you recognize, the familiar syllables *do, re, mi, fa, sol, la, ti, do (ut)*. You will notice the order of these vowels, so arranged because they belong to different families. The family is determined by the part of the mouth primarily responsible for the vowel or mold, and as the only movable parts of the mouth are tongue, lips, and jaw, these will be our vowel families.

- *i* (mi) and *e* (re) are molded by the tongue
- *a* (fa) is molded by the jaw
- *o* (do) and *u* (ut) are molded by the lips

The Lost Art of Bel Canto

One thing is common to all vowel molds. The tip of the tongue rests *lightly* against the lower teeth. This keeps the tongue from closing off the throat. The sensation of enunciation of all vowels is about half way back on the tongue. This spot on the tongue will be more *forward* for some vowels than for others, but must *never be back* on the tongue. If allowed to be back on the tongue and, therefore, back on the mouth, there could be no acceptable pronunciation since the act of vowel formation would leave the tongue and be performed by the throat.

The following chart may be helpful in visualizing the forming of vowels.

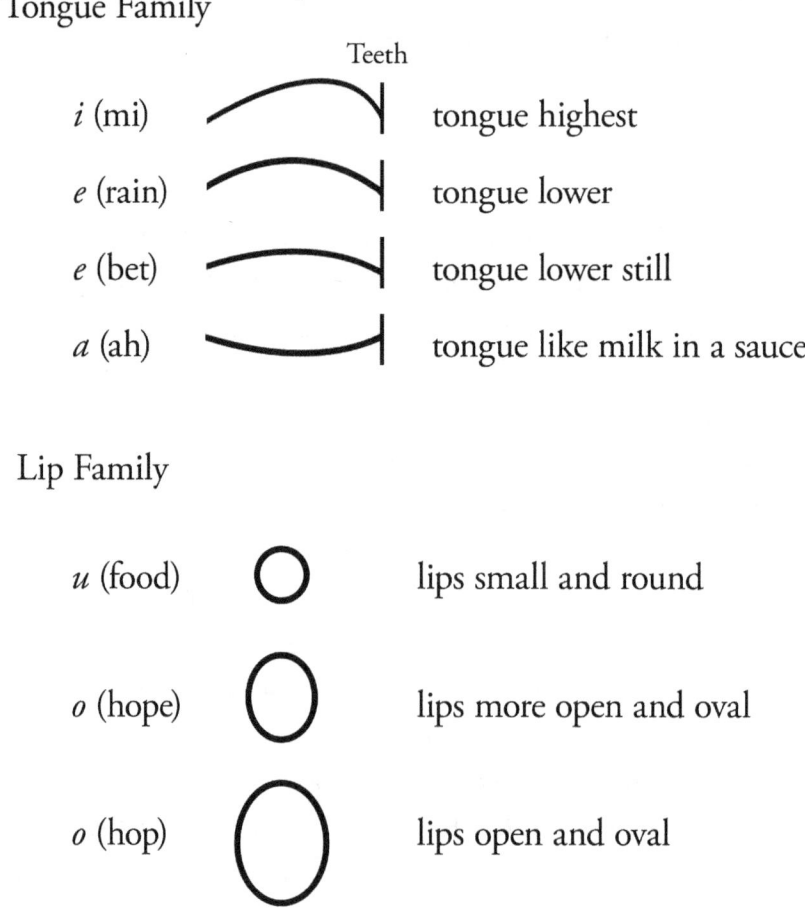

It should be remembered that any mold has sides as well as a top and a bottom and a little firmness at the corners of the lower lip against the lower teeth rounds out the mold.

The test for the correctness of the molds for singing is the sensation of pronunciation precisely like that of correct speech. Any deviation from the natural unaffected pronunciation will show up in distorted and unpleasant sounds. Though it is true that the molds *i, e, e* (and French *e* mute) require less space between the tongue and the roof of the mouth than do the dark vowels *o, oo, ah, aw,* the amount of space must not be controlled by depressing the tongue, but by lowering the jaw.

Try it. Sing *ah* as you would speak it. Your jaw will be dropped considerably and the vowel will be natural and pure. Now, as well as dropping the jaw, consciously depress the tongue and the vowel becomes distorted and muffled.

It might be well to explain what is meant by dropping the jaw. There are two ways to open the mouth: one, by a tensing of the chewing muscles and the other by relaxing these muscles. The latter causes the jaw to drop in line with the normal bite. This is what we mean by dropping the jaw.

The vowel *a* (Italian of course) is a dropping of the jaw and a relaxing and opening of the throat, which requires no consideration except by the ear.

Serious defects in pronunciation lie in allowing the vowel to anticipate the following consonant. ("It is human to rrrrrrrrrrrr." —W. L. W.) This usually occurs on the final consonant. In languages other than English, final consonants are spoken as a syllable, not overemphasized or stressed but clearly articulated. Such a practice is not amiss in singing in English. Here again, however, it must be re-emphasized that exaggeration of any kind in singing is a fault and that all suggestions contained in this book are within the bounds of natural, not affected practices.

Consonants take various positions and movements which are indicated by clear articulation.

Faulty diction, indulged in by most singers, results from incorrect placement of vowels and/or lazy lips and tongue which fail to provide clean, clear, and crisp consonants. All consonants are formed without changing the mold of the vowel which they accompany and can for a high degree of flexibility of mouth muscles.

Covered Tone

The Italian method for *bel canto* or "beautiful singing," was and is based upon the use of the covered tone and it is without exaggeration to say that there has never been a great singer who did not use the covered tone.

It is also true, however, that most present day teachers are scared to death of the term, partly because they do not understand what it is and more because of the muffled woolly sound which they incorrectly attribute to it.

Actually, the covered tone is a tone which results from the air-stream striking the hard palate in line with the eyes and it is a free, rich, beautiful sound capable of infinite varieties of expression.

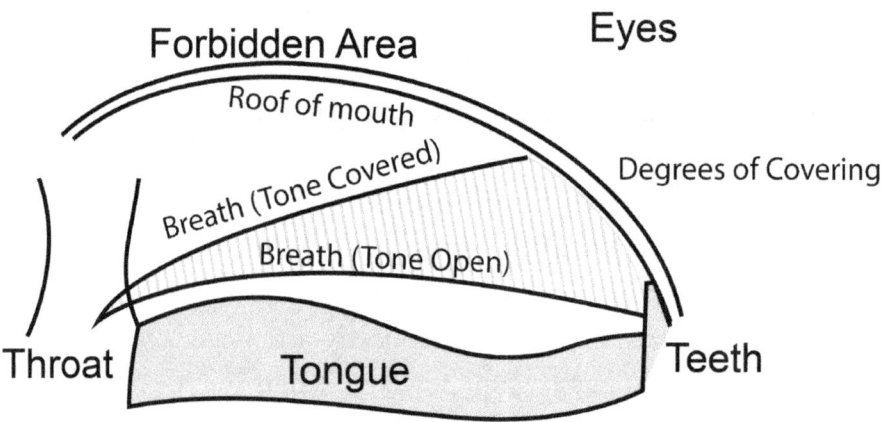

The illusion or sensation of shortening the mouth or the roof of the mouth is accomplished through a feeling of tallness from the crown of the head which in turn tends to aim the breath column at varying points on the hard palate. At no time in singing is it defensible to close off the nasal passage. This is probably understood, but bears repetition.

The method by which William L. Whitney built beauty into voices is based upon the use of the covered tone. Its validity needs no justification for it is only necessary to hear the hundreds of pupils who have worked with him and to hear the characteristic quality and control of their voices to know that the correct use of the covered tone is the foundation of great and successful singing.

We shall now endeavor to clarify the use of this tone in voice building. In a former paragraph, you were introduced to the term "mounting the breath," (*montare il fiato*) and promised an explanation of its use in singing. In order to cover the tone, or point the breath stream at the eyes, we do two things, namely, (1) feel tall from the crown of the head, and (2) mount the breath. The two things are done simultaneously. The actual mounting of the breath involves the action of the diaphragm which has the effect of lifting the breath from the stomach to the chest, while slightly inclining the head. (Whenever this term *inclining head* is used, it is understood that it is a result of the illusion of tallness or straightening of the neck, rather than the actual tipping of the head forward.)

When To Cover

The art of singing lies in knowing when to cover and when not to cover, and there are quite definite rules to guide the singer. There are only three possibilities in melody: (1) it goes up, (2) it goes down, (3) it stays where it is. This is referred to in this book as the *build of the melody*, and from the build of the melody we draw our first rules for covering.

1. *When the pitch descends*, the descending tones should be covered. There is no exception to this rule. By so doing, the tone emerges without diminishing in quality and is amply supported, much as the waterfall which constantly tumbles with strength and direction out and over, to the pool beneath.

2. *When ascending by a series of skips of a third or greater*, attack the upper tone covered, sustain it less covered. Here we have an exception. If the upper tone of the interval is a climax, then we cover the tones which just precede the top note and attack the top note from the covered position and then release it within the bounds of good tone. It will not be a yell, or completely open because the preceding tones have given it position.

3. *Ascending by step as in the diatonic scale.* The scale is made up of a series of whole and half steps, or semi-tones. In a slow ascending scale, the singer covers the semitones,

particularly the lower tone of the interval. Remember that this is for scales taken at a *slow tempo* where there is plenty of time to cover.

4. *With rapid scales* it is entirely different. Here our rules for covering are entirely evolved in behalf of quality, intonation, and flexibility. They involve:

   a) *Graded breath flow.* Graded breath flow is almost self-explanatory and means a metering out of breath by the diaphragm to meet the demands of the build of the melody.

   b) *Cross of the voice (croce della voce).* Cross of the voice needs explanation. It refers to two positions of the mouth, namely the smiling position and the round position. Neither position may be forced or artificial but must be absolutely natural. By so doing, the *quality* of the tone changes but *never* the vowel or mold.

   c) *Systematic use of covered and normal tone.* The systematic use of the covered tone and normal tone in rapid scale passages involves the graded breath *flow* and the cross of the voice. The following illustration will help you to understand. Use the vowel *a* as in "far."

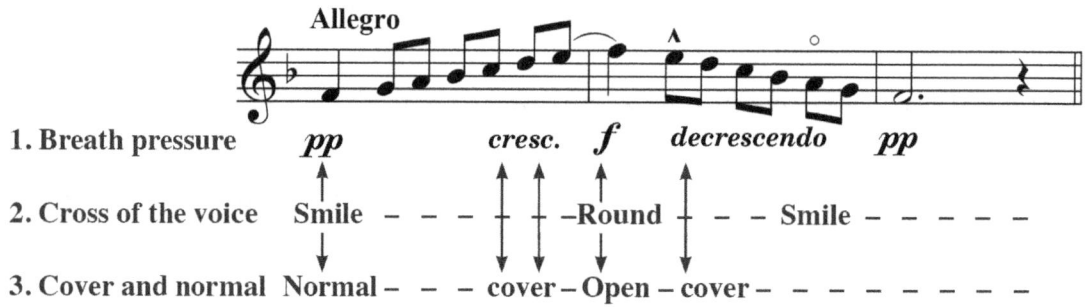

In analysis, the preceding illustration means that the singer begins with a well-supported PP, (not covered, but normal with the mouth in a smiling position). At "⌒" mount the breath and cover. On the high note, or climax, breath flow for forte (means *strong*, not loud), tone free, normal and full (not covered), mouth is rounded, well-opened position. As you mount the breath, slightly incline the head (act of covering) and maintain this position to the end, keeping rounded mouth position to **o**. At **o** breath flow for pianissimo, still covered but mouth position changes to smile. Try it rather slowly until you get the idea and then remember that all rapid scale passages, if handled in this manner, will be clear, even, and untaxing upon the voice. For in this management of florid passages you have the secret of the remarkable grace, control, and clarity of the singers following this method. It soon becomes a singing habit and the student finds no difficulty in applying it to the melody in hand.

I have said that this approach to florid passages is untaxing to the voice: Most of you are too young to know anything about the horse and buggy days, but if you are ever country-minded and enjoy walks or rides through New England, you will find old roads that climb a bit, then level off, then climb some more and level off again and so continue to the top of a high and taxing hill. These level stretches take the load off the horses and give them a respite which allows them to climb steadily to the top without fatigue. So it is with the handling of the voice just described. The covering and smiling rests the voice for it seems almost like a suspension of the work of singing and so allows for a reserve energy and breath supply to be applied to climaxes and/or long phrases.

5. *When the pitch is repeated or the melody stays where it is*, the tone-placement (covered or normal) depends upon where the sustained pitch falls in the voice, and upon what is to be done on that pitch. This leads us into a new technique called *messa di voce*. (Do not confuse with *mezza voce* which means half-voice and is the name given to effective singing in soft voice.) *Messa di voce* is the art of taking a tone from a *pp* attack through a *gradual* crescendo to a forte climax and then back through a *gradual* diminuendo to a final pianissimo without losing the tone-placement or having any bumps or interruption of quality and sound. It is the highest peak of artistic singing and an uncommon accomplishment among even the finest singers and yet it is within the grasp of all who have the patience and the knowledge to develop it.

Upon *messa di voce* depends the elasticity of the voice. It is easy to sing loud all the time. Such singing demands no skill and is often just as good before as after training. You have all listened to fine voices and doubtless have been a bit envious of the size of the voice until you realized that the singer could not sing softly; that when he attempts soft singing, the result is a breathy, muffled little sound utterly divorced from the quality of the forte singing. Such a state is a serious flaw in method of production and/or the inability of the student to comprehend. It is seldom the latter, for the good teacher will not permit lack of comprehension on the part of his students. When do we use *messa di voce* and how is it used? We use it in *all* singing which means that we use it most of the time.

How is it accomplished? The attack of pianissimo is smiling, mouth placement normal followed by a mounting of the breath and slight inclination of the head (covering), a gradual opening of the tone and increasing breath flow to the climax, which is free and normal with mouth well-opened and full breath flow, followed by mounting of the breath and slight inclination of the head (covering) to tapering off with smiling position of the mouth, light breath pressure to the final pianissimo.

Example:

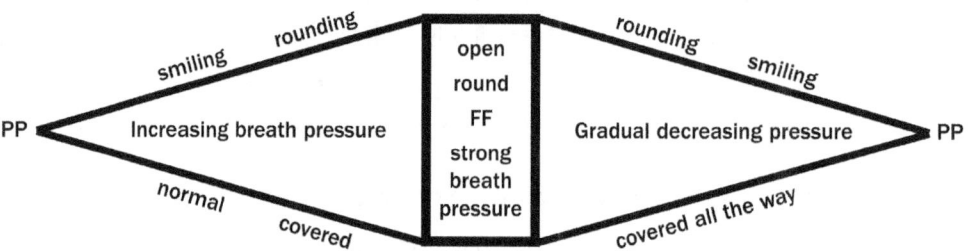

In this one difficult but attainable accomplishment, the entire method is brought to bear and we have the ultimate of any method in singing—namely, quality, perfect intonation, and flexibility.

The Act of Singing

The act of singing involves several steps and considerations which I shall try to state simply.

1. Take a low breath (as described on page 16) through the mouth.
2. Diaphragm acts to exhale or expel air. (Remember, the sensation is one of pulling rather than pushing the diaphragm up.)
3. Breath causes the vocal cords to vibrate.
4. Breath with resulting sound travels on through the throat until it hits something.

5. The only thing it can correctly hit is the hard palate or roof of the mouth. The tongue drawn back or the stiffening of the throat muscles or the wrong position of the head are the possible obstructions to the tone hitting the hard palate, and must be eliminated. This hard palate is the keyboard of the voice.

6. The breath (tone) hitting the hard palate will set up vibrations within the resonance chambers in line with the place where the tone strikes the hard palate.

7. The quality of the tone is determined by the place where the breath hits the hard palate and the resonance chambers so activated. Since there is no human mechanism for changing the direction of the air-stream, it is necessary to move the target and this is done through the position of the head. For example:

    a) The head is tipped back so that the open mouth is practically in line with the breath stream. The result is a yell, devoid of color or quality, white, bland, and unbeautiful.

    b) When the head is held in normal position, the breath stream strikes just above the upper teeth and we have a good tone, colored by the resonance of the frontal cavities.

    c) When the head is ever so slightly inclined (not tipped forward as is a common misunderstanding) the breath column strikes the hard palate in line with the eyes and sets into vibration all the head resonance chambers. This results in a tone of great richness and color which is essential to beautiful interpretation.

    d) Allowing or making the breath strike the hard palate at varying places between the front teeth and in line with the eyes, produces tone of varying qualities.

Try it and see. Tip your head back and sing a tone, and then, without changing your production in any way, move the head back to normal position and on down until your chin is on your chest. This brings us to a very important point. As the head actually tips down, that is, after the column of air hits back of the line of the eyes, the tone becomes muddy, muffled, and sounds as if there were a hot potato in the mouth. Such a position with its resulting tone is not acceptable and should be avoided. One of the most difficult accomplishments of the artist is the ability to judge the placing of the tone so that it will meet the interpretive and melodic demands of the music without going too far in either direction.

Posture

Every student asks the question, "How shall I stand to sing?" To give specific instructions to such a question would be unwise and yet we know that posture has much to do with both tone-production and making contact with one's listeners. A slumped, lazy position, be it standing or sitting, will impede the breath, both in inhaling and in controlling its expulsion. Such a position robs the resonance chambers, particularly the chest, of their rightful functioning. This posture produces flabby, ill-supported tone which is usually entirely off the breath, and therefore muscularly produced. Not only is such a posture harmful to good tone-production but it is also very bad to look at. The listeners will be quite sure, and who can blame them, that the singing will be insecure, sloppy, and apologetic. Who wants to listen to such a performance?

On the other hand, rigidity of position and posture resulting from muscular effort is equally restricting and offensive both to the eye and to the ear. Tension will pinch the tone and inhibit flexibility for it will interfere with the free handling of the breath and the relaxation of tongue and jaw. There is, then, a happy medium where the position for the singer is neither sloppy nor rigid, spineless nor tense. The weight should be balanced between both feet, one of which is placed slightly forward of the other. This prevents strain on the muscles of the abdominal wall and allows for support of strong singing. It is also a graceful and attractive stance and so serves two purposes. The body should be erect, with the chest comfortably high. It is a mistake to throw the shoulders back with a mighty heave and assume a West Point position. On the other hand, it is wise to develop straight shoulders and the resulting chest position in order to make way for resonance and breath and to assure a naturally commanding and confident appearance. We have mentioned the position of the head in a former paragraph and so here we need only mention that the head should not be "held" in any position but should assume the position necessary to the build of the melody. It should not, however, take an extreme position either of being thrown back or tipped down on the chest. Since the singing makes demands upon the entire body, the posture of the body must be such as to allow for support, control, and flexibility. Therefore avoid extremes of any kind and work for that happy combination of relaxation and alertness which might be called poise.

Pitch

No consideration of beautiful singing would be complete without attention to that *must* of all musical performance—good intonation. Natural endowment in ability to hear correct pitch varies. In fact, it runs the gamut from sensitivity to the most minute variance in pitch to inability to distinguish between pitches of a quarter of a tone in variance. For the latter, many would say that good intonation is an impossible accomplishment but such is not always the case. A faulty ear perception is serious and makes the study infinitely more difficult. It presents a serious problem, particularly to the singer, who must produce a given pitch entirely subjectively without any of the mechanical aids present on other instruments. While good intonation is, in the last analysis, a matter of the ear, there are aids in the tone-production which will help the student.

The most obvious of these has to do with muscular forcing of the tone. Just the minute the tone is produced through pinching, and so lacks proper flow of breath, it becomes rigid, hard, unbeautiful, and deviates from true pitch. Such deviation may be slight or gross, but the very rigidity of the tone inhibits the fineness of the pitch adjustment. Such a tone is like forcing a ball against a hard wall without a chance for rebound. This cannot happen if the tone is free for such a tone always hits the roof of the mouth rather than the throat and having resistance and rebound, it becomes tone by virtue of the motion set up in the resonance chambers, not by virtue of muscular determination. Therefore, rule number one for good intonation:

> *Do not force the tone or allow the production to be muscular. Maintain the breath as the supporting factor in all singing.*

In developing good intonation, practice with a "light tone." You will notice that I do not say "soft tone." The beginner will almost always associate "soft" with a pinched, swallowed, small sound, utterly divorced from the quality of the full voice. Any restriction or lack of support will interfere with good intonation and so the term, "lightly" which elicits a concept of freedom and airiness plus quality, removes the restriction and aids in pitch adjustment. It is easier for the student to *hear* the pitch when singing lightly than when singing full voice, and since the development of the ear is a major task in good intonation, it is only sensible to give the ear every possible opportunity. This is not to say that the student should never sing full voice, but we are here concerned with developing a concept of good pitch and the light voice helps. Rule number two is as follows:

Sing lightly and listen constantly to pitch.

Attention to the placement of the tone will also be of great assistance to good intonation. Descending passages that are allowed to drop back into the throat (which seems to be their natural inclination), will err from pitch however slightly, particularly in a pianissimo but also in a forte. The mounting of the breath and the placing of the head so that the breath stream hits in line with the eyes results in a support which overcomes the tendency to flat. Such a tendency will not, of course, be overcome in a moment or a day or even a year, but the adherence to this manner of singing will greatly aid in the security of pitch. Rule number three:

Adhere to the habit of covering all descending passages.

Another place where good intonation comes a cropper is at the climax or high note. This may be due to two things: (1) tension, either psychological or physiological, and (2) faulty preparation. If the tone or tones preceding the climax are covered, the tone which is the climax is placed by virtue of the preceding position and may be sung freely and strongly without fear of spreading over several pitches. Remember that the covering of the preceding tone involves the mounting of the breath which acts as an insurance policy to the climax and automatically provides it with the needed support. Rule number four:

Cover the tones preceding a high note to ensure correct placement of the high note. Usually take a high note with mouth well opened and in oval position. Don't forget the slight pressure of the corners of the lower lip to the teeth. (Regola della croce).

If the breath is allowed to hit against the throat instead of passing through the throat and hitting the roof of the mouth, the tone will be flat. Remember always that the throat is merely a passageway through which the breath gets to its quality-producing target. The only demand made upon the throat in singing is that it keep out of the way — in other words, that it not be closed so that it will interrupt the breath-stream before it reaches the correct placement. Rule number five:

> *Never allow the throat to close and thus attenuate or narrow the breath stream.*

In summing up, good intonation results where bad habits in singing are eliminated. Good intonation persists when the ear is sufficiently keen to demand meticulous accuracy of pitch. Consistently good intonation comes with correct management of the breath which implies good tone-production. There is no short cut to these accomplishments, but through patient and intelligent practice, good intonation is within the grasp of all normal people.

Registers

The Italian method upon which Mr. Whitney's method is based, does not countenance isolated registers. By that I mean the artist sings evenly from the lowest to the highest note in his or her range without a change in voice. There will naturally be a deeper quality where the chest acts as the main resonator (chest register) than in the upper tones where the head resonators are responsible for the quality, but beautiful singing does not show any break or sudden change of quality between registers.

The human voice is all one instrument, embracing five octaves, contra G to 3-line F, comparable to the keyboard of the piano. We call it *bass — baritone — tenor — contralto — mezzo soprano — soprano*, and find that part of this keyboard is produced by male voices, part by either male or female and part by female alone. The following chart will give a clearer picture of this one voice. The registers are physiologically determined, but are traditionally named "chest," "mixed" or "middle," and "head."

The Lost Art of Bel Canto

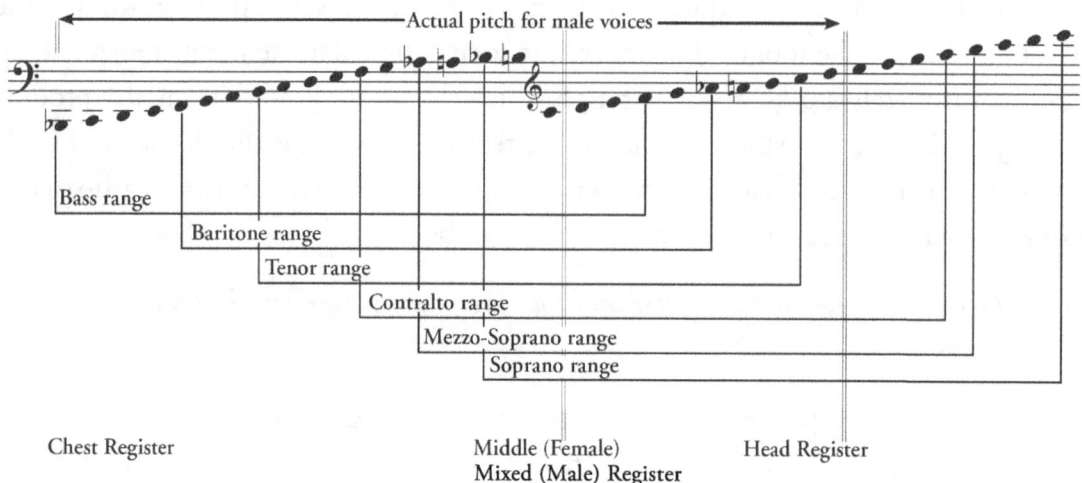

A first consideration of this chart of adult voices reveals that:

1. By analysis, all voices employ the chest register, the lower voices using it more than the higher.

2. All voices use the mixed register.

3. Only female voices use the head register.

A second consideration shows us that:

1. The changing tones from chest to mixed registers in all voices come around *small B flat, B natural, C,* and *D*. Some male voices may need special attention to tones as low as *small A*.

2. The change from mixed register to head comes for women's voices only. The crucial tones for all types of women's voices come around *two-line C, D, E, F*. Some singers have more difficulty with the *C* and *D*, while others may need special help as high as *F* and *F#* and *G*. Since it is not our belief that the knowledge of physiology of the voice is in any way necessary to the development of beautiful singing, we will not go into the changes of the vocal cords which accompany the several registers. It is, however, vocally important to realize that at the point at which the voice leaves the lower and enters the next higher register, there is great tension upon the vocal mechanism. For this reason, it is vocal suicide to force the lower register up. In other words, to

sing one-line *D*, *D#*, and *E* in the chest register puts terrific strain upon the vocal cords and results in forced, insecure sounds which seldom are in tune. On the other hand, it is *not* harmful, but indeed quite acceptable, that the upper registers be carried down through the changing or crucial notes.

Just as the vulnerable spots in a spliced rope are the points at which it is joined, and the strength of the entire rope depends upon the smoothness and length of the splice, so the points of change of register are the crucial points in the smooth and even line of the voice. This means that particular care must be given to the tones involved. The method which I am endeavoring to present in this book meets this problem through covering the *"changing tones."* The essential of freedom from forcing and strain is thus met, for the mounting of the breath and the placement of the tone in the covered position gives quality without pressure and welds the registers smoothly and evenly. Again, it must be stressed that the covering should *never* be excessive or unnatural, and the minute the student gets a muffled, hot-potato-in-the-mouth tone, he is placing the voice incorrectly. These changing notes or notes marking register extremes are always weak in the voice and there is too often a tendency to hammer away at them on the theory that exercise strengthens. Such a theory is dangerous because it is a half-truth. Exercise does strengthen, but it can also wear out a delicate mechanism unless it is intelligently and correctly applied. The development of registers as such will never produce beautiful singing. The skill and art of the singer is to so use the voice that the registers will be taken in stride and so fused that the listener cannot know that they exist. Such is the result when:

1. Lower registers are never forced up into higher.
2. Higher registers are carried down into the two or three tones of the next lower register.
3. The changing tones involved in the adjacent registers are sung lightly and covered.

It is my good fortune to have notes taken at the lessons of many of Signor Vannuccini's pupils, and out of the wealth of experience and wisdom of his teaching, they might well be put down as beacons in the difficult task of producing beautiful voices. I shall quote them exactly except that I shall translate them from the Italian in which he spoke.

1. Singing on the throat impedes high notes.
2. Don't tinker with the larynx. Trying to lower it takes the brilliance out of the voice.
3. Open your mouth (heard at every lesson) but do not stretch it.
4. A natural position *always* results in the best tone.
5. Intervals attacked from underneath instead of from above will be flat. (Here he always gave the illustration of the bird alighting on the branch rather than the bat that swoops up and hangs under the branch.)
6. Avoid any contraction or stiffening of the body or person.
7. For the trill, feel the accent in the head.
8. Avoid using too much breath pressure on descending passages. It hurts the pitch and wastes the breath.
9. Sing frankly and confidently.
10. Avoid the sound *aw* for *ah*.
11. Demand of yourself and do not be *pigra* (miserly).
12. Tremolo often comes because the breath touches the throat before it hits the roof of the mouth. To avoid this, practice the scale by aspirating the first note, then smile, cover the seventh, open everything on the high note. There will be no tremolo if the voice is correctly placed.
13. Have your mouth open *before* the attack.
14. On extremely high notes, sometimes use a smiling position.
15. Stop making faces. If it hurts it is wrong.

In working with a voice, it is best to use exercises of short compass and carry them only to the pitches which are completely comfortable for the voice. To stress the extremes of the voice is tiring and unnecessary, for the growing understanding of how to handle the voice is the goal of the student and that can best be achieved in the easy part of the voice. Once the student gets this "feel" of the voice the extreme notes will fall in line and become as easy and natural as any other tones in the range.

The Method

It was always Mr. Whitney's belief that once the singer learned *how* to sing and could recognize a good from a less good tone, he need not worry about the extremes of the voice or its size.

A serious consideration in the music world today is the unreasoning and quite stupid emphasis placed upon big voices. The general public mistakes size for beauty and anyone who can yell loud enough is a great singer. Unfortunately, too many of our present-day music critics know no better and also put a premium upon loud singing. Does the answer lie in giving them what they want—coarse, loud and often unbeautiful singing? Perhaps, but such is not the thinking of Mr. Whitney. The greatest art of singing lies in the ability to handle the voice gracefully and effectively so that the singer is capable of all the gradations of the dynamic scale. It is a matter of proportion rather than strength of molding the phrase so that the climax is achieved on the volume scale of which voice is then capable. This can be accomplished by exercising with the light, easy, natural voice, but will *never* develop if the exercising is done in a loud, heavy voice with an eye to volume. As the student matures both physically and artistically through the experience of singing, the voice will also mature and sufficient strength or volume will be forthcoming. Volume which comes from pushing beyond the natural strength of the voice may bring a momentary illusion of bigness, but the voice so abused will soon wear out and the "success" will be short lived.

This must not be interpreted to mean that weak, anemic, puny singing is to be encouraged. The light tone, (no matter *how* light) that is correctly placed will always have quality, vitality, and meaning, and if such is not achieved, then the production is faulty. It may seem like a voice crying in the wilderness, but it is our earnest hope that young people will discriminate between tones that are just loud, forced, and muscular, and tones that are full and rich and buoyant (on the breath), and will recognize the latter as the valid volume for which to strive. Is the miniature less beautiful than the mural, or the watercolor than the oil painting? The answer lies in the skill and judgment of the artist, not in the size or medium of the product. So it is with the voice. Whatever your voice may be, the determining factor in its beauty lies in the skill with which you handle it, and the moods which you create through it, not in its range or size.

Studies and Exercises

The achievement of the three musts of good singing, namely: *quality and elasticity, flexibility,* and *accurate intonation,* demands long and careful practice. This practice should be intelligently carried on, with the student always aware of the intention of the exercise on which he is working. Actually, no two voices are equally served by the same exercise and it is for this reason that no one can develop the voice by reading a book or by singing all the exercises therein. However, since this book will be used mainly by those who have been pupils of Mr. Whitney, or who have been taught by his pupils and are therefore able to choose among these exercises, I shall include those which he used most often in his teaching.

Along with exercises specific to the needs of each pupil, he used several studies extensively. The Whitney Vocal Study was Vaccai, *Practical Method of Italian Singing*. Every Whitney pupil was led carefully through and then pastured in Vaccai. Each study was carefully marked by Mr. Whitney, to show the exact demands upon voice management, i.e., where to cover, where to smile, *messa di voce*, dynamic contours, phrasing, etc. Vaccai was used in the first lesson and continuously used to the last lesson for all of us.

Other studies which he used with enthusiasm were:

- Panofka: *24 Vocalises, Book 1*. This was particularly valuable in developing flexibility and as used for soprano, alto, tenor, and bass.
- Lütgen: *Book 1 for Velocity*. Used occasionally.
- Righini: *Sofeggi, Book III*. Used extensively for basses.
- Concone: *50 Studies*, and *25 Lessons in Singing*. Used sparingly.

Still others were: Abt's *Tutor*, Aprile, Bordogni, Nava, and many others. Since going through Mr. Whitney's library, I have found over sixty different studies, all carefully marked, and evidently used to solve the vocal problems of some particular pupil.

Studies and Exercises

It might be worth mentioning here that all such material with his markings will now be available, as his library has been placed as a gift in the library of the New England Conservatory of Music in Boston, Massachusetts.

<u>**Key to markings in exercises**</u>:

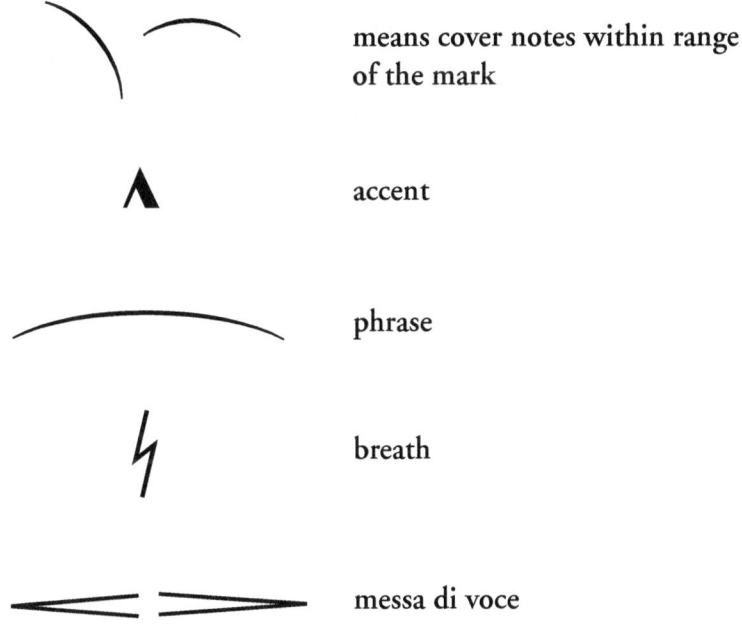

The Lost Art of Bel Canto

To develop even vocal line

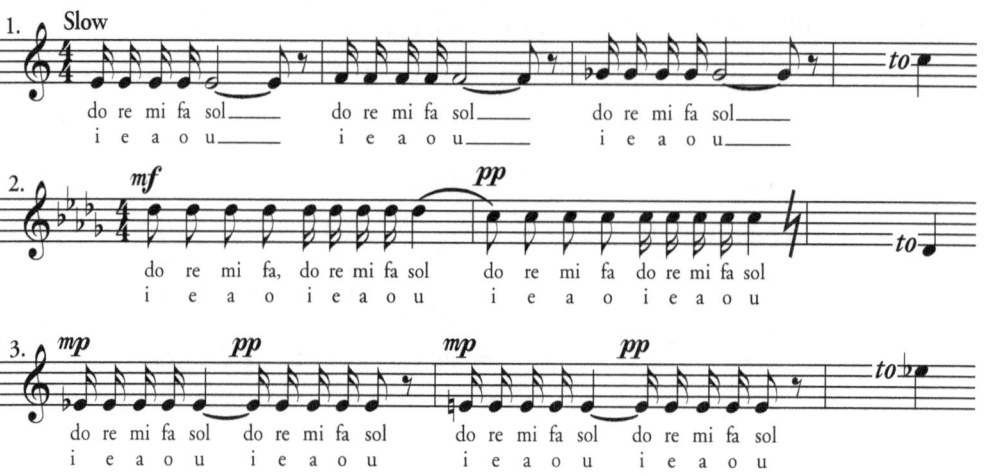

For controlling and sustaining tone
Cover where indicated

Studies and Exercises

For maintaining vocal line with changing vowel sound

The Lost Art of Bel Canto

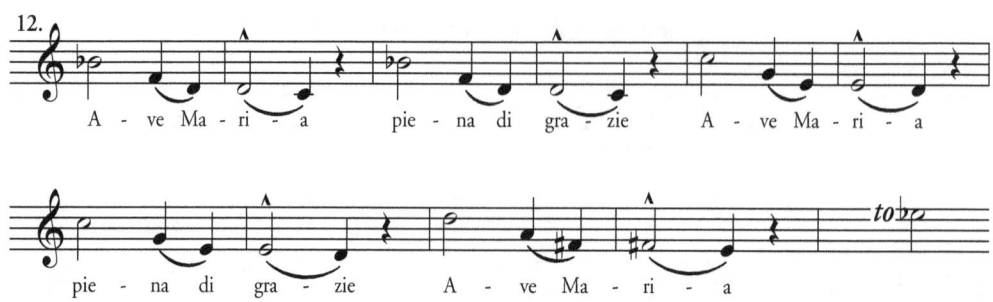

For breath management through covering grouped notes.
Cover all descending passages; ascending where marked.

Studies and Exercises

The Lost Art of Bel Canto

For Messa di Voce

Studies and Exercises

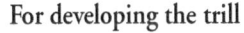

For developing the trill

The Lost Art of Bel Canto

To develop flexibility for florid passages (Handelian runs)

Studies and Exercises

For use of: (1) Graded breath pressure
(2) Covered and normal tone
(3) Cross of the voice

The Lost Art of Bel Canto

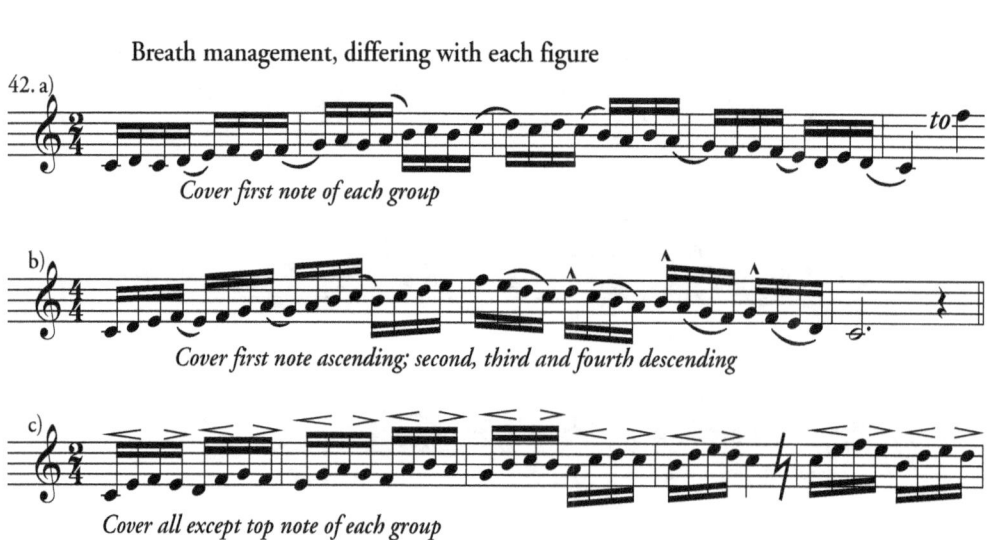

d)

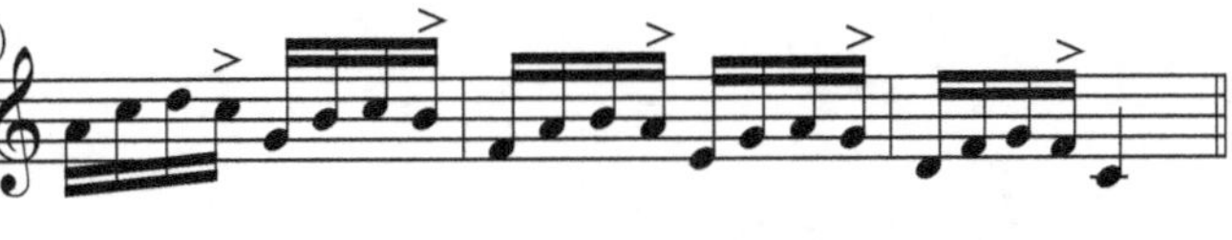

43.

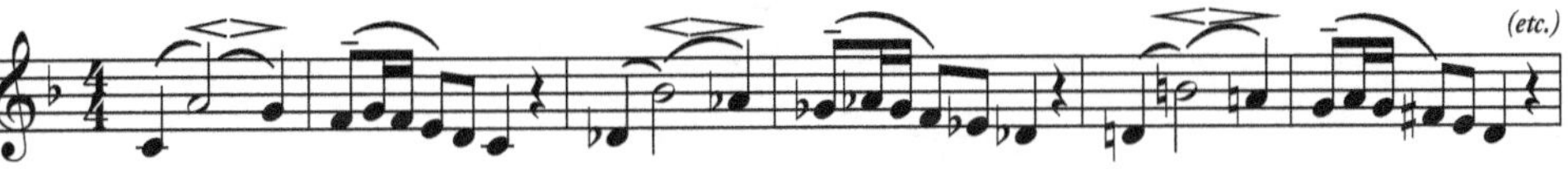

44.

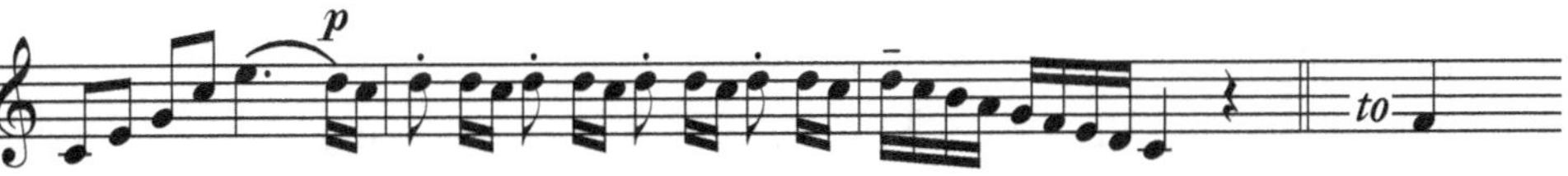

45.

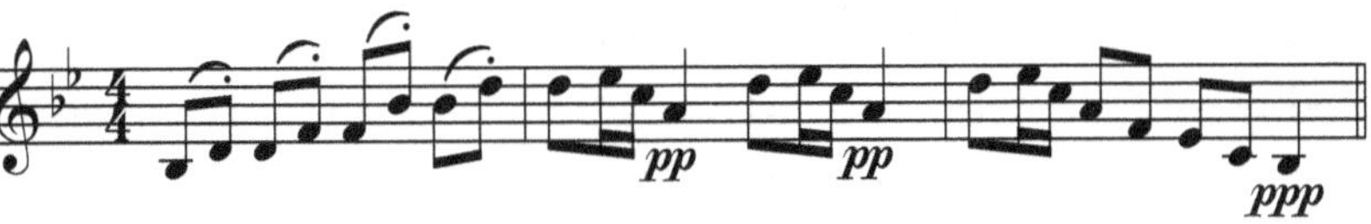

ascending by semitones

46. a)

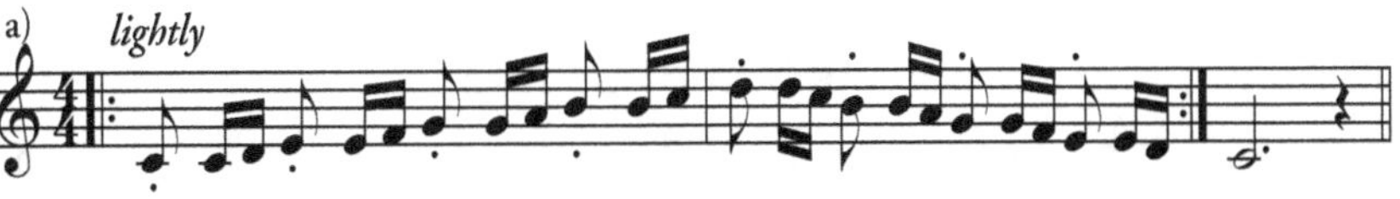

Twice in one breath

b)

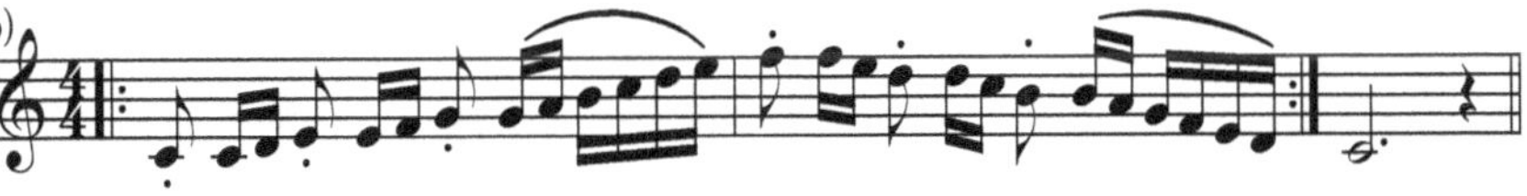

Twice in one breath

47.

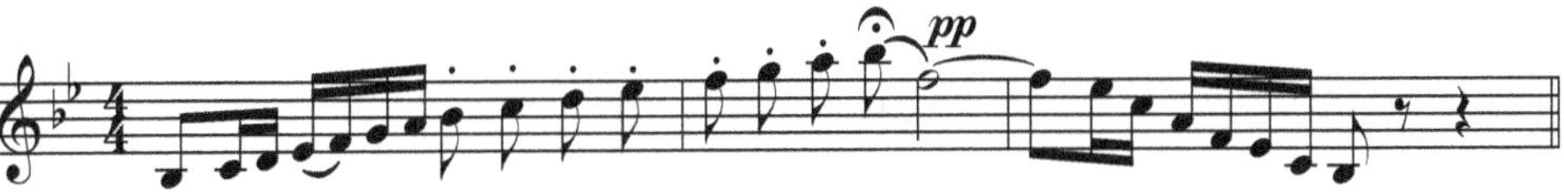

Scale endings

48.

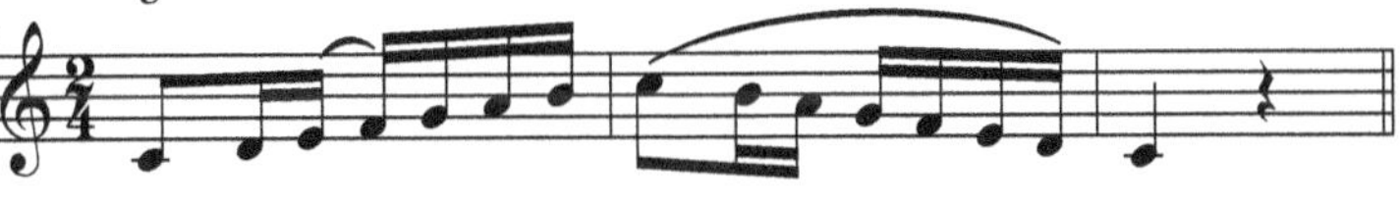

Babbo

by William L. Whitney II

Babbo is approximately "Daddy" in Italian. Something I presumably gurgled as a baby must have sounded a bit like that. Mother was staggered that I could speak a foreign language at that age, and wasn't about to let that idea get away. Therefore, I called my father "Babbo" throughout my youth and until he died.

He was probably not a "great man," although there were a good many people who would consider him such. He was, at the very least, a wonderful man. My grandfather, Myron was a great singer, considered by many to be the finest bass America has ever produced. I have read in a biographical publication on him that his musicianship was of course to be expected, since his father played the harmonica in church. My great-grandfather was an adventurer. In 1810 he went West from the traditional family home (since around 1640) of Watertown, Massachusetts—admittedly with the cooperation of his parents, he being seven at the time—and wound up in Ashby, also Massachusetts. They figured that was far enough. There was no sense in overdoing things.

Although my grandfather spent his childhood in Ashby, he returned to Watertown while a youth and studied music in Boston. There he married my grandmother, Eleanora who is rumored to have kept his nose to the grindstone, and receives considerable credit for his very successful career. My father, William Lincoln, born in 1860, was the first of their three children, followed soon by Lizzie Gertrude and quite a bit later by Myron William, Junior. That poor soul was known as Junie throughout his life. I have a program for an 1873 recital featuring, among other delights, a Beethoven "polocca" for piano, four hands, played by Miss Lizzie and Master Willie Whitney. That implies a relatively cooperative family situation. They were apparently normal, however. I also have several letters of the 1870s from Eleanora, who was in England on concert tour with Myron, one of which notes that she is greatly disappointed to learn that Willie has not been practicing appropriately and has even been (gasp) arguing in the parlor. He should understand that they have not bought his present yet!

Those old letters are wonderful to have. There is, perhaps, a bit more emphasis on religion and behavior than we would now expect, but relationships are certainly not much changed. They sound quite modern with some exceptions. Grandmother reported that some of her new friends were fascinated with people from the "frontier." One of their children was curious to know if her children were black, or maybe red. My grandfather was ill while in England, and that was a much bigger deal than it would be now. He recovered, and his tour was a great success. I have a program including him singing in London's Crystal Palace. The letters can also be beautiful. Grandmother's hand looks just like copper plate engraving. Grandfather's emphatically does not. And his letters are about 10% as long as hers. No doubt this results from early sex stereotyping.

When Babbo was a little boy, he was watching a stone mason carving one day. A splinter from the chisel flew into his eye, blinding it. In those days the only treatment known was to place leeches on the eyeball, in hopes that they would draw the sliver out. They did not succeed. My father's eye turned white, and he was most sensitive about it when young. I believe that was a prime reason that his later career turned to teaching voice, rather than performing. He was reputed to have an even more beautiful voice than had his father.

One characteristic, shared by every male member of my family of whom I know, is extreme—perhaps morbid, shyness when young. Most of us overcame this in time by learning to put on an act, or acts. My own shyness lasted through college days, to a point that I avoided answering the telephone, since I didn't know what would be expected of me if I did. My father never did fully conquer his.

Babbo studied piano and singing in Boston and later in Italy and Germany, with teachers who had coached his father before him. He developed an enviable reputation but simply couldn't pursue performing at the level needed. Such is a vocation requiring incredible drive, particularly if you lack a wife like his mother to do the driving. I have a letter home from him to Eleanora in which he fervently hopes that she and his father will not be too disappointed, but he simply cannot be a "great man." All was not gloom and depression, though. He bicycled all over Italy on a bike with a huge wheel in front and a little one in back. There are also letters to one Florence Roberts assuring her that he will never amount to anything. She ended up marrying him anyway.

He studied and taught in Europe for some years, and founded the *William L. Whitney International School for Vocalists and Pianists*, with branches in Florence, London, Paris, and Boston. I regret not having been around in those days, although his wife of that time probably would have objected, at that. He would take American students for a year's study in Europe, centering in Florence. The total cost was estimated to range between $1,250 and $1,600, which "could hardly be exceeded except where students are extravagant in the way of living." This included the round trip voyage ($150) plus two weeks in Spain, Gibraltar, and Morocco ($88); ten days in Naples ($50); ten days each in Venice and Rome ($45 and $50); and return to Florence via Sienna ($30); as well as living arrangements for the year in private houses, lessons, piano hire ($2 to $6 per month); music; and attendance at concerts and operas. My half-brother, Harry, had arrived some time before, and he got to sample the travel.

In the course of his work in Europe, my father did some charity recitals, one of which had him well down a program with Franz Liszt as the headliner. He also met and discussed matters with Brahms, and did some coaching with Gounod. Those heady days ended, unfortunately, with the First World War. Several of his faculty were lost in the fighting, the schools were permanently closed, and he returned to America and taught in New York and Boston. He and Florence agreed to disagree. Harry stayed at home with her and Babbo moved into his club, *The Saint Botolph Club* of Boston. That was what a gentleman did in those days, at least in Boston, when a marriage faltered.

I know little of those days, although small bits of light peek through, now and then. The family was comfortably well off. Babbo was doing famously, and Florence was the daughter of a family who owned a chain of drug stores in Italy. Harry married Marie Schillander, a great cook of whom I became very fond later. "According to Mother," a caveat to which I shall be forced to refer now and then, Marie's father was a distinguished Swedish gentleman and her mother had been his cook. Florence's family were not thrilled at the cook part, so when they passed away a considerable bit of money was left in trust for Harry's and Marie's son, Karl, with only interest available to his parents. "According to Mother," that was to preserve it from Marie, in case she didn't turn out quite right. All I know is that Marie and her parents were lovely people, and I loved them when I knew them. I know that Harry and his family, including his mother, spent time on Cape Cod and in Florida, since I have an adventure story Harry published about a flivver trip between, entitled "Fording the Atlantic Coast." Babbo, Harry, and myself were all addicted to puns. From some tapes Karl made with his parents, it is clear that they made a happy family and the Schillanders, including uncles and such, were delightful.

My mother studied singing at Russell Sage College, along with the cooking, sewing, and such expected of girls. When she graduated she went to New York in hopes of continuing her studies and pursuing a voice career. Her teacher suggested she look up Mr. Whitney, to that end. She looked up an ex-Metropolitan tenor of whom she had heard, instead. He charged her $60 for an audition and raved about her voice, promising to have her well launched in no time. Mother was not stupid. She had vocal hopes, but not *that* many illusions. Telling him off in no uncertain terms, she left in a huff!

She was pretty broke, but went to see Mr. Whitney, anyway. He asked her to wait a few minutes and gave her a couple of three year old magazines. She sang for him. He was complimentary, not effusive, and accepted her as a pupil. She asked how much she owed him and he said he usually charged $60. However, she had been sent by an old pupil (her college teacher), so that dropped it ten or so; and she was just out of college, so that certainly dropped it another ten; and she hadn't found a place to live in New York, so that certainly should be considered. On the whole, she had better get out of there before *he* owed *her* too much. That sounds just like Babbo as I knew him; no caveats there!

Mother advised me that my father had led a lonely life after his first wife died and that he, after many years, had finally found her (Mother) and lived a rewarding life again. From letters I found and a few other sources, it appeared that they were married quite shortly after Florence died, and that Mother had traveled abroad for a year or so on a scholarship provided entirely by him, before that. By whatever route, all ended well, if on a bittersweet note. They were married in New York in the presence of his brother-in law and one of her two sisters, and no one else. I arrived, saving the day with her family and somewhat improving things with his. But the 1929 crash had arrived a few months earlier.

My father, previously quite well off, lost everything he had in the way of finances, and all assets except a cottage on Cape Cod, which wasn't worth anything to anyone else. He had an apartment in New York City, on which he could not break the lease. Not surprisingly, aspiring singers who could afford lessons were not thick on the ground. Things looked pretty bleak, but again I saved the day. My parents had, I firmly believe, a good marriage, but one that was really just getting under way. I have a love letter written to Mother by Babbo when I was a month or two old. Characteristically, it was ostensibly addressed to me. May and late November relationships are not famous for long run success, but with a very small family addition and virtually no money, there was no choice.

A way had to be found to exist and grow. They finally did get out of the apartment commitment, and moved to Massachusetts.

The Cape Cod cottage was made livable. Falling plaster was patched with old sheets dipped in flour-and-water paste. The hand pump in the kitchen was primed and made usable. The outhouse was intact, if not alluring. Kerosene provided for light and cooking needs, and the fireplace for heat. Babbo made an agreement with The New England Conservatory of Music to chair their Voice Department and, thanks to his reputation, to keep all money he earned teaching there. Everyone else was broke, too, so Mother managed a deal with a bank to get a more promising house in Newton, close enough for bus travel to and from the "Con" and life started anew. I continued to squall and carry on, without the slightest idea that there was any problem. It was always that way; nobody ever told me anything.

That is not quite true. When I was a little boy, Mother told me to sing in the junior choir at church, which she directed. Naturally, that was torture. Mother did a lot of things at church. I felt, and feel that she was one of their prime suckers. Babbo didn't go to church. From several quasi-reliable sources, I heard that he had been through all that. He had been brought up Episcopalian, and had tried several other denominations, supposedly including Catholicism and Judaism and finally, I presume, Atheism. He came to church on Easter Sunday and sat in the back long enough to hear Mother and me do the junior choir bit, and then left. When I was not rehearsing for that duty, he met me after Sunday School and we walked home, about a mile, past a lake into which we threw rocks. I enjoyed those walks. I think I recall, possibly with Mother's help, one of the Pastor's visits to our Sunday School class, during which he asked how many of our fathers went to church. Not all that many, as it turned out. He was not surprised; he recognized that fathers were very busy people, and often needed their rest on Sunday. I assured him that was not the case with Babbo; he used to go, but had just gotten tired of it. My religious education was left entirely up to my mother. Possibly that's one reason I ended up with my father's beliefs—and I still like to throw rocks into lakes.

My father was truly remarkable in his sensitivity to people and his handling of them. I came to understand that somewhat during his life, and much more later through contacts with his pupils and others who knew him. There was usually an element of humor in his approach and, superficially, it looked simply like joking. But the result was nearly always an easing of some problem for the person with whom he was dealing, or a strengthening of their relationship. He rarely seemed to offend anyone, even though he sometimes appeared to risk that. One of my best friends, who is now in his mid-nineties, told me of his first meeting with Babbo. He was a young singer who wanted to study with Mr. Whitney. To that end, he arranged for an audition and brought what he has described as some very pretentious Beethoven songs. My father took the music and accompanied him, as expected. When finished, my friend, Kenneth, anxiously awaited the decision—Babbo told him that yes, he would accept him as a pupil. As he was leaving, happily delighted, Babbo said "by the way, young man, before you do that again, I think you should get Beethoven's permission!" Kenneth broke up laughing. They became fast friends, with my father taking a strong position of mentor, as Kenneth later did with me.

My father was a brilliant accompanist, and always played for his pupils when they made their first recital as part of their training. Normally, it was given at the Conservatory's Jordan Hall before a good many friends, relatives, and even a smattering of paying public. One could count on the young performer being terrified. He or she would stand in the curve of the grand piano, greatly resembling a piece of statuary. Babbo would be seated at the piano, and would test it by playing a few chords. Unsatisfied, he would peer into the case, remove a handkerchief from the tail pocket of his cutaway, and stuff it into the instrument. Another test would still present unsatisfactory results, so he would repeat the procedure. This would go on until the audience—and the performer—were chuckling in a relaxed manner. Then the recital would proceed. I do not recall his ever running out of handkerchiefs before the desired result was achieved.

Babbo was also one of the kindest men I have ever known. Most of his pupils were pretty low on funds, working several jobs in order to study at the Con. Quite a few had scholarships, at least for their voice work, which were really just his refusal to take their money. They never knew this, during or after their studies. My mother, who helped him with his accounts, knew—and told me—about the practice, but no one else was let in on it. Sadly, that led me to a most unjust view of my mother's kindnesses. She did them in the open. I thought that didn't really count. I was very wrong. Over the years, I have learned of many, many generous acts of hers, beyond those I knew of then, and of the warmth given and received in the process. That closeness was something Babbo probably couldn't have dealt with. They were both wonderful in their different ways.

That extraordinary shyness should not be underestimated. In spite of a remarkable sophistication and a wisdom certainly not available to younger people, there was a lurking difficulty in his close relationships due to the residual presence of that characteristic. My mother's cohorts from the church were not of great interest to my father. Nonetheless, they were important to Mother, and some support from Babbo was to be expected. After considerable debate (read *pressure*) he agreed to come home rather early and meet her friends one evening when they had met at our house. He didn't show up. Mother was frantic. After her friends had left, she called the local hospitals and such—after all, he was in his mid-eighties by then—and finally drove the entire route to and from the Conservatory in case he might be stranded somewhere. As she pulled into our driveway after a fruitless search, the car lights passed over Babbo, asleep on the back steps to our house. He simply hadn't been able to face meeting all those people, none of whom he knew or understood. I feel a considerable resonance with that. My mother, however, felt nothing of the sort, and was quite understandably furious. She left him to sleep the rest of the night right where he was.

We had a small hyperactive cocker spaniel named Frolic. For the first few years after we took him over from a relative who was moving and couldn't really handle him, he would leap on anyone who paid attention, frequently peeing in excitement. Before we acquired him, he had been kept outside in a doghouse. Friendly people were a big deal. In time, he matured to the point that he leapt, but (usually) controlled his bladder. My Father came home from work at night, usually around ten. On occasion, I was allowed to stay up and greet him. I don't know what happened on other nights, but when I was there, Mother would make a big thing of kissing Babbo hello. Babbo would make an equally big thing of yelling for the dog, who would leap up and down between them. I don't know whether I was being entertained, or Babbo just didn't go for all that mush.

Babbo was concerned, I later learned, that I was brought up too much under the influence of women. That was inevitable. My mother's mother lived with us, since my grandfather on that side had died very soon after I was born. Her being there was actually a boon to all concerned. Since Babbo was elderly when I came along, it had to be accepted that Mother one day would have to assume responsibility and provide for the family. To that end, she took a second degree, her first being in home economics or something considered equally appropriate for a young lady of her time.

She earned a Bachelor of Music in Music Education at the Conservatory, did all the practice teaching and other preparation, and became accredited in the public schools. Then she went on to a Master's in Education from Harvard. She chaired the Department of Music Education at the Con by the time she did have to take over the family. Later, they granted her an Honorary Doctorate. To put it mildly, she was a busy woman. My grandmother, Neenie to me, helped with the home and with me. Mother was very much involved, however. So was Babbo, although he believed that Mother was generally in charge where I was concerned.

Mother was pretty good about letting me grow up with broad experiences, but she tried to protect me from the world in a few ways. She decreed that I would never be allowed a BB gun. My father provided one shortly thereafter. She felt that the streets were getting too busy (her reaction now would be full blown hysteria) and that I therefore *must* do without a bicycle. My father bought me the only English bike in our area. Mother was a good sport; she helped me to learn to ride it. At least she could absolutely prohibit any guns in the house. On my following birthday, I found a twenty-two rifle in my bed. Mother taught me to shoot it, and turned out to be a crack shot, herself. She also acquired some belated wisdom and issued no more ultimatums. My father felt I was protected enough.

I was pretty much the standard young pain through my teenage years. In fact, I was a late bloomer, and stayed pretty worthless well into my twenties. I wish very much that I had gotten to know Babbo when I became an adult. I know it would have improved my life and I am sure it would have been a pleasure to him, as well. As it is, most of my values came from him, whether or not I managed to adhere to his standards. There was never a need to consider honesty, certainly not its technical aspects, because he was an honorable man. My mother was helpful to just about everyone, as a decent Christian woman—more correctly, a remarkable one. She never allowed differences of race, or religion or any other group identity to affect her treatment of anybody. But for my father, no such distinctions existed at all. He was fully secure as to himself; he was spared the concerns that come from religious beliefs. He was a human being, and so were those with whom he dealt. That was fully sufficient.

Babbo died during my sophomore year at college, over Christmas vacation. I really wasn't able to face that, and was no help at all to my mother during that sad time. I pretended it wasn't happening and told no one, acting among my friends as if all were normal. On the night he died I had a date to take a friend's much younger sister to a dance. We kept the date. I felt, perhaps foolishly, that canceling out on the very shy, very uncertain, very young girl was simply impossible. My obligations to my mother should have been much more important, obviously. Those to myself for that matter, should have had almost equal precedence. I was pretty much a mess.

Babbo's last few days were spent essentially in a coma, and at home. He kept his humor and his character to the end. On the final ride home in the hospital ambulance with Mother, he rallied enough to ask the driver to blow the siren. Each time Mother or I entered his room he pulled himself out of the coma to acknowledge us and see to our feelings. One day before he died, he put out his hand and shook mine, quite formally, and said, "I'm proud of you, old boy!" I won't forget that, or him. And nobody I know who ever met him has forgotten him, either. Perhaps he was a "great man," at that.

William L. Whitney and his wife, Leta Fulton Whitney
Source: *The Neume*, 1949, New England Conservatory Archives, Boston, MA.

Andy Anselmo

www.ingramcontent.com/pod-product-compliance
Lightning Source LLC
Chambersburg PA
CBHW080414300426
44113CB00015B/2520